Millionaires
secret
Know L'Edge

What you need to know to generate unlimited wealth

Tomy Shaw

DEDICATION

This book was put together to give the reader the most value per dollar spent. I've researched a lot of ways to make money and lost a lot of time and money on that journey.

I genuinely believe that this book represents the knowledge of a wealthy person.

I always loved sharing my knowledge and have always been very curious, especially for the truth.

Applied knowledge is indeed power and freedom
The truth will set you free
The more you learn, the more you earn

These three quotes have been repeatedly in my head, and they helped me stay motivated and focused.

Experience gathered over the years

I am a real estate investor since 2011. My method is to buy and hold, with positive cash flow from the start.

I have been investing in stocks since 2014, technical trading, and some fundamental analyses.

Chapter 1: Inflation

There are two main drivers of asset class returns - inflation and growth.

Ray Dalio

Some might ask, what does inflation has to do with millionaire's secrets? Well, in this chapter, my goal will be to demonstrate the effect of inflation on assets, liabilities, and how the wealthy utilize inflation in their favor.

$$Wealth = ((Assets/Capital) \; X \; (1+Inflation)^N) - (Liabilities \; X \; (1-inflation)^N)$$

This formula states that assets gain value when inflation is above zero and that liabilities lose value; we must remember that it reduces the cost of money.

Here is a simulation of wealth on a million dollars of assets with a ponderation of 80% liability, in the formula, we did take cash flow or income into account, over ten years, 200 000$ in Equity, would now be worth 528 094.36$.

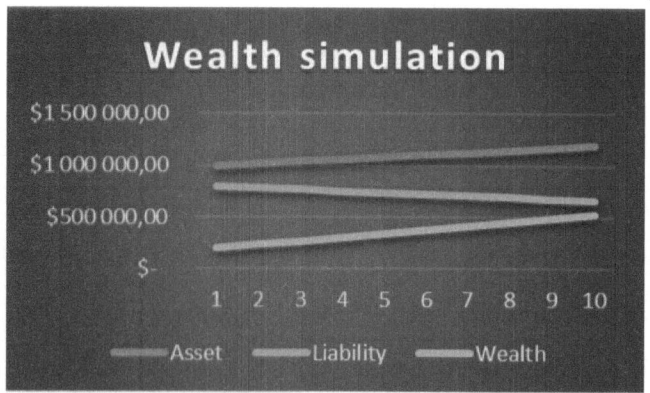

An excellent example of how inflation creates wealth; of course, this example does not take into consideration the cost of borrowing money.

And it is to be noted that low inflation seems to create even more inequality. (PE ratio tends to jump to higher multiples in a low-interest environment). *More on this later.* Understanding this principle will significantly enhance your ability to create wealth and financial freedom.

Chapter 2: Cap rate, ROI & Leverage

Leverage can be very powerful or very destructive.

How does cap rate, return on investment, and leverage come together?

Cap rate (%) = (Net operating income / Asset price) X 100%

Cap rate is the return that you get on your assets.

Now, ROI is what you make on the money invested; if you paid cash for the total asset, then your return on investment would be the same as your cap rate.

By using leverage, it will in thus increase your return on investment, but also increase your level of risk.

ROI = Cap rate – (liability/Asset) X interest on the loan) X (1/% of down payment)

The formula states that leverage increases the return on venture when using debt in your investment, for this formula to work, the asset returns must be higher than the cost of the mortgage.

Note: Return on investment can be positive, but have a negative cash flow, more on this later.

As stated, the return on investment.

ROI = (Net operating income / Capital invested)

Chapter 3: Pay off your debt

Personal debt is slavery.

I know this looks like I am contradicting myself but let me be direct; debt not attached to any generating source of income is just plain stupid.

Here are some examples of bad debt, car loans, boat loans, and credit cards.

One of the main reasons why I emphasize paying personal debt is the interest on that loan isn't deductible. The interest paid will be based on your net income after being taxed

Paying debt is also the safest investment one can make; it is inflation hedged, and interest saved on payments of debts is not taxed, reread this last statement for a better understanding.

If you do not have lousy liability, then what I would recommend buying real estate and then paying off that mortgage, for any reason, this suggestion might offend some, but cashflow is just too important in my opinion, cash flow is the foundation of financial freedom.

We all heard of growing businesses that make significant profits but all unable to collect the cash of clients and or even pay the minimum debt payment required.

Chapter 4: Marriage & Savings

One of the pillars of power: unity

I have always been afraid of marriage, but once I got married and started working on our financial freedom, our wealth exploded in value.

It might not seem reasonable since we were not able to save double, but approximately ten times our original amount that we were saving per month before unity.

You must keep in mind that most of the monthly expenses do not increase by that much, rent stays about the same, the cost of foods stays about the same.

Now that you start to acquire some equity, banks are willing to lend money at lower interest, buying a home becomes possible and even investing in real estate.
Long term effect of unity = Wealth and freedom.

It is the same concept of a corporation, corporation unite many people with different skills and thus increasing the power of the corporation, which results in wealth accumulation.

I think that the takeaway, is unity, since unity becomes power, and for potential to exist, there must be accumulation and control.

Chapter 5: Intrinsic value & Fixe expensed

Fixed expensed are the egos friends — Tomy Shaw.

Most want to look rich, so they buy everything on credit, the ego loves this, but will demolish your spiritual self.

Freedom is on a spiritual basis.

In finance, we always attribute intrinsic value to perpetual income, that was an epiphany for me since we assign value to something that come in regularly, but what about fixed expenses, could it have an intrinsic value.

No courses in university were ever teaching on this subject, and I decided to analyze it for myself.

The results concluded where astounding, in my opinion, of course.

Fixed intrinsic value = Fix liability cost per year/interest on capital wanted by investors.

We could use many examples to help you understand this concept, think about it in terms of anything that you make regular payments every month. The fixed expenses can be a car, a boat, or even an oven stove that you pay regularly.

Say, you have a car payment of six hundred dollars per month and that investor want a five percent return on their money, well you would take 600$ X 12 to put the amount on yearly basis, then you would divide that number by 0.05 = 7 200$ / 0.05 = 144 000$, the car intrinsic value would be of 144 000$, since, you would need 144 000$ to make 7 200$ in returns at five percent interest.

This example does not include inflation and taxes your income. If so, the number would be even higher, making the value of that car very expensive.

Chapter 6: PE Ratio

Wealth creator

The wealthy genuinely understand the price to earnings ratio. It is one tool that utilizes in their wealth creation.

Price to earning ratio = Price of the asset / Earning

The inverse of this formula is the cap rate or the returns of the asset. The ratio indicates the value of your newly net income created multiplied by a number determined by the sector in question, all area of activities will have their multiple, the higher people think that the industry will have growth or stability of revenues, the higher the number will be, this also called the hype of the sector.

This ratio only applies to assets that generate profits or can produce it in the future. It can't be used to personal income, the PE ratio of an individual is zero, since if you stop exchanging your time, your income vanishes, so does its value. It is one of the reasons that the rich don't work for money.

PE ratios can vary and somewhat dependent on a sector of the economy, and some fast-growing tech companies can get as high as 100X times PE, one dollar in net income per share, is worth a 100$ in value. It is the power of price to earnings ratio.

Businesses take advantage of this, and sometimes the company will sell 1$ of equity for 100$. Therefore, companies love to sell their shares to finance themselves. Remember, the seller on average wins.

It is also one of the reasons that it does not take money to make money, and it takes knowledge of how wealth is created. For example, many businesses start with nothing, then they grow the business, hirer new personal and acquire assets that contribute to the growth of the company, then one day, the profits of the industry get to a hundred thousand, but if we were to look at the value of the business and say that the P/E ratio of that sector would be of 10, then you would multiply 100 000$ by 10, then the value of the company would be worth 1 000 000$.

This concept is so powerful, since, no money was saved, all money was invested, but still, the company is now worth 1 000 000$. Imagine a person wanting to save a million, and they would need to make 10 000 000$ in order to save 10% of their income, to keep a million. This also why the rich don't save money, they created.

Chapter 7: It's still possible

Be strong, be fearless, be beautiful. And believe that anything is possible when you have the right people there to support you. — Misty Copeland

Wealth is possible for anyone who desires it, key words; one must actively want it. One must be able to develop all the attributes necessary for success, in other words, one must acquire success habits and the right knowledge, I genuinely believe that this book will enhance your ability to understand wealth and to create it.

Working on oneself will give you more and more energy, you start to notice, that you do not resonate with people anymore, since people on their night off wants to watch television and you, on the other hand, will want to work on your projects. This motivation will make you feel motivated to work on your dreams, what you focus on, you will experience in your life.

Setting big dreams will make you feel scared at first, and this feeling is healthy, it is because you are stretching above your comfort zone. Your body is telling you that you have a lot to learn and your body is making up more energy, and you will need to learn how to use this energy productively since the knowledge will dissipate the fear and in the process, you will become better. When becoming better, that experience will be transformed into confidence in yourself and the world.

When you genuinely want something, it pulls you towards it, and in the process, you are beginning to be happy about yourself, you must appreciate every steps, since you are attracting exactly what you want, the resistance of experiencing to the present moment will cause you pain, but one must know, that the present, is what you genuinely wish to, all you need to do, is have faith in the moment and then you will experience, joy, since, you become aware of the fact, that you truly create your life.

Only fear can get in your way; in abundance, there is no fear, there is only passion and love of what you are doing.

Joy is an internal feeling, it can not be bought nor experienced by taking something, it is always there, and it is there abundantly when you become grateful.

So, it is still possible, when you choose to go trough, this going through and to appreciate the moment, will cause you to create wealth, this wealth will be in your hands. Remember, all is possible; all you need to do is believe.

Chapter 8: The process of becoming

The mind is everything. What you think you become. — Buddha

Most people want to become wealthy but are unwilling to become the person that makes money and thus acquiring the ability to keep it. First, you must love what you do; if not, you will not endure the race; remember, wealth is a lifetime goal. Doing something that you hate just for the money will make you sick. Never work for money solely; work on who you are becoming. Don't be a salesman for cash, be salesmen for the attributes that you will gain by becoming one and at the same time acquiring a paycheck, get my point?

In anything you do, learn to value money but not work for it; if not, you will spend it in disorderly fashion. When you value money, you will want to protect it, so the preservation of capital is essential. Then when you preserve your wealth, the next step is learning how to invest it, what to expect, and what kind of investor are you? What is your niche and easily accessible knowledge of your sector?

It is a part of my life that I usually made a mistake, I was focusing on a million dollars of net worth, and I wasn't focusing on the process of who I was becoming. When you see yourself evolving and becoming a better person, this will motivate yourself to want to continue.

If you concentrate solely on the goal, you will feel empty inside and won't be able to be grateful for what you already have, and ungratefulness will push you to try to skip some steps, like gambling your way to wealth, we all know that this process is unstable and will not work.

Chapter 9: Money problems are just the symptom

An investment in knowledge pays the best dividends – Benjamin Franklin

Lack of knowledge, education, and experience will lead to money problems. Not knowing how wealth is created and how money works will lead to poverty. If one does not have any education, he will be forced to work at close to minimum wage, since the minimum wage has a hard time to cover the monthly expenses to live, this leave the person no other exception to take on debt to get by, since he has no capital or ability to save it, no resources will be working in his favor. Even the debt that he has acquired become a burden in the future.

Lack of experience will diminish his hourly wage, and lack of knowledge will prevent him, even though he might have capital, but the simple fact that he cannot earn interest on his wealth, will lead inflation to demolish his money, resulting again in poverty.

Capital is necessary, but how to get it, takes experience and knowledge, it is not required to save it, if one knows how to buy undervalued real estate, many people will want to be aboard, but again, most people don't have the knowledge on how to manage and invest in real estate, so money does not show up for them.

It is why I state, and money problems are just the symptom, the real cause, is lack of knowledge and experience.

Chapter 10: Odds of success

Work like hell. I mean you just must put in 80 to 100-hour weeks every week. This improves the odds of success, if other people are putting 40 hour work weeks and you're putting in 100 hour work weeks, then even if you're doing the same thing you know that you will achieve in 4 months what it takes them a year to achieve. —

Elon Musk

The quicker you can fail and move on, the faster, and you can stack the odds of success in your favor. So many people are afraid of making a mistake that they never try anything new, or a non-conventional way. Since they are terrified, they find themselves looking for a secure job, but what wealth can they accumulate? Well, the only way they can create wealth is through saving and investing. Wealth is created but at a fraction of what they could do, if they knew how to create.

By learning and trying new things, this increases your chances of growing rich, since you are no longer scared of failing, now this leave you with an immense energy to focus on what you want to create. The faster you can create the business and delegate it; the faster wealth becomes attracted to you. Remember the P/E ratio; this alone explains why the rich get richer; they firmly understand this ratio.

Most of the times, if the criteria are respected, the company can be sold without paying any capital gains. Always consult your accountant; remember, they have a lot of years of education. Do not minimize their knowledges.

Also, the simple fact that one exposes themselves to success increases their chances of attaining it. Since the person will be reading more books, achieving seminars, and dealing with people that want the same results will program his mind on attracting people that have success, thus increasing his odds of success again.

Having long term goals will also increase your odds of attaining the outcome desired. Every choice will have concurred with your long-termed goal, thus increased your chances to accomplish it; people with short term goals, usually dissipate all their energy in many directions. Since, when one goal is done, they will take another goal, but this new goal could be in the opposite direction of the last goal, so you moved forward and to finished to where you started.

The long-term goal will ensure that all short-term goals are linked with long term one.

Chapter 11: Failure leads to success

Success is the ability to go from one failure to another with no loss of enthusiasm — Winston Churchill

In my experience, playing it safe, never leads to success. Real estate, stocks, and businesses all have risk involved. Learning how to deal with risk/rewards reduces risk. To minimize this risk factor, one must learn how to manage it.

Failure is only overcome by persistence and courage; character diminishes the power of failure.

Every time I made a lot of easy money, I became weak, and I lost most of my motivation, but every time I lost a lot of money, it would make me stronger and more motivated, I would do a lot of the thing that I didn't want to do, since my desire to succeed was strongest at my lowest point.

When you encounter a loss, you also must face it, most of the times you thought it was a great idea, but until you act on it, you won't know for sure, so I feel that it constructed a better and more realistic map of reality, which enabled me to take better decision from that point on.

It gave me the ability to sharpen my vision. It made my beliefs brighter and better, living a fantasy world is very easy, sometimes I listen to people, saying that if they had a million dollars, deals would quickly come to them, this information couldn't be further from the truth, if you have a lot of money, people want you to get involved in their bad deals, and they don't care if it goes sour, since it is not their money. I also thought, that if I invested a lot in the stock market, it would be easier to become rich, well I learned this the hard way, and lost a lot of money, even if I was committed.

When you fail, it will hurt, since it usually makes you face the truth that your ideas were not as good as you thought they were. Failure may lead to a significant loss of money and time. It happened to me many times where I had invested into a stock that I believed would explode in value, to find myself loosing half of my money. The pain was so great that I felt like isolating myself and just being depressed, but the real winners get back up and askes this question, what can I learn from this experience?

Even some knowledge that you think is useful can be useless unless one tries it for itself. I usually say, if you can't make money with your experience, well it's because it isn't worth anything.

Chapter 12: Are you excited by your goals?

A goal should scare you a little, and excite you A LOT – Joe Vitale

When you are working at your job or on a project, were you excited by it? If not, you are probably doing it for the wrong reasons. If money alone, becomes the sole purpose of your life, this probably means that you aren't living, and believe me, I fell in this trap many times. Every time money or net worth was my goal, and I became unhappy because I didn't appreciate what I had, I was focusing on the future and not the present or in the process of what I was doing.

The only way you can know if you are going in the right direction is to follow your heart, and your heart gives you a feeling of joy when you know that you are moving toward the ideal person that you wish to become. It will be hard, since, some will try to control your thoughts and actions to the conventional way of thinking and acting. But you must always remember your hearts desire. I am not talking about your cravings or bodily desires; I mean your spiritual desires that make you grow as a person.

There is always the easy way, but the easy way is usually the wrong way, unless it is aligned with your spiritual pathway, what I mean by the easy way, is that let's say you want to write your book, but instead you decide to watch a movie series, well you know deep down, that this action is not moving you towards your ideal self.

We all have this inner compass that helps us navigate through our lives, but sometimes it can be hidden by a lack of emotional intuition, only when you listened does it become stronger, sometimes you will have answers in the middle of the night. You must act on these impulses, they will guide, and things will happen, and now you will not understand, but in the long term, you will be able to pieces the puzzle together.

Once the pieces start to fit together, there is joy that will flow through your body, and you will say thank you because you will know that sometimes higher is guiding you to grow and helps you to become the person that you are meant to be.

Chapter 13: Play the game to win

If you want to play the game and win, you've got to play 'full out.' You've got to be willing to feel stupid, and you've got to be willing to try things that might not work — and if they don't work, be willing to change your approach. Otherwise, how could you innovate, how would you grow, how could your discovery who you really are? — Tony Robbins

Capitalism? If one takes the time to notice that in the word, capitalism, is the word capital. So fundamentally, to understand the game of capitalism, one must understand the meaning of capital. Investors capital is essentially the equity in a business or even the ownership of an individual.

Capital gives access to debt, the more that an individual or corporation has access to liability, well the more he can acquire assets, and assets are the real producers of wealth, since for example, if you have 50 000$ of capital and that you would put that money in a mutual fund, if the mutual fund had the ability to give a 10% yearly, well the maximum you could make on your capital would be, you guessed it, 10%.

Now let's look at another example, like in real estate or a business, the return on capital is always in direct correlation with how much leverage you can acquire, if it only takes 20% down, well you can borrow the other 80%, say now the asset in question, where to produce a 5% return, well since you have a leverage of 5 times, well it will a lot more profit on the capital invested. It would be 25% approximately since one would have to pandurate the interest on the debt.

A big mistake that people usually make is to protect the little account that they have; this is the mindset of fear and doubt. To win at anything, one must have a great offense plan. An abundant mentality will push you to increase your revenues or sales.

There are always two sides to a coin, obstacles, or opportunities. If you concentrate on the expense, you are trying to protect yourself, while if you see a chance in the barrier, you will see and seize the moment.

One time, I had offered some assistant to a friend, his company was burning cash and had a net loss, his strategy was to cut expenses, so he took his two prospects and he made them work full time on trying to minimize the costs, the simple fact that he concentrated on cutting expenses, created more fees, as the saying goes, energy goes where attention goes, a this really made me think. We attract what we believe.

I told my friend, what I had noticed, and then went on to say, you should focus on doubling your revenues, and that would, at a certain point, create profits.

Chapter 14: Intemporal value of money

Invest in inflation, it's the only thing going up — Will Rogers

Currency loses value with time, some people aren't willing to invest, but what they are not aware of or maybe they are, is that, it is perilous to stay in cash, it is hundred percent sure, that the currency in time will lose value, they say that stocks are risky and that real estate is also, but either way, it is always dangerous, whatever decision that you take, you must learn to welcome risk, it is part of life.

It is always risky, but they are degrees of risk. Using leverage in the stocks is very risky and downright suicidal. I know that we do not talk about risk when something is a positive outcome, but for me, I mean dangerous in the sense that you know that with time, the value of the currency will fall, so it is better to learn how to welcome inflation. By welcoming, this will push you to learn how to minimize it at least effect to zero.

Buying gold would be one way to protect the capital that you have saved, but gold will not generate a steady income, this will not give you financial freedom, this is why that you should keep on finding creative ways to invest in assets that generate income plus are inflation hedged.

Now, what is the probability that you lose money when you buy a new car? A hundred percent sure, unless you are a professional car salesman. So, since the chance of losing money, is a hundred percent sure, well we don't call this risky since the outcome is assured, that what's funny about risk. If the result isn't sure, well, we call this factor risk.

We should try to ask the question in a way that can help us in understanding how we can not only protect are capital but question that can lead to the ability to increase it. Therefore, in the bible, it is stated to him that hadeeth the more will be given, since, he has acquired the knowledge to make it grow.

Currency must always be converted into today's value, and a good financial advisor should be able to help you, with this process, since it might be hard to comprehend at first. Inflation is a very complicated subject; there is a lot more about inflation and deflation than just price variance.

Chapter 15: Power, love and truth

The past cannot be changed. The future is yet is your power —

Unknown

These are the three central aspects of one life, power, is your ability to make the right decisions, love is your ability to follow your heart and truth is your ability to find the answers that you are looking.

When one has become influential in the spiritual sense, money will accumulate in his life, and it will be converted into his net worth, I truly believe this aspect of life. I do not think it is a coincidence. Falling into temptation or instant gratification will lead to poverty, but when one has learned how to manage these emotions, it will become easier to accumulate wealth.

Love will give you the courage to face obstacles, if you do not love what you do, fear will lead your life, and you will be unable to accomplish your desires, when you like what you do or people, you will try to help them by offering something of value, you will try to give them as much value for the price you are selling your product or service.

Truth is truth, and your spirit knows when it has heard it, it can not be argued or debated, it is like this question, are you alive? Well your soul knows that is alive, there is no arguments that can state otherwise, well this is the same in your life, when you hear something that does not feel right, well your spirit knows that it is not the truth, the more you listen to your soul, the closer you will become to the fact.

The truth will set you free, and I genuinely believe that when you know the truth on how freedom is created, in time, you will become, if you are wise enough to take the right steps to acquire it. You can know the truth but not apply, I would call this folly, and if you do take the right steps with the proper knowledge, this will indeed lead to wisdom.

Chapter 16: Spend less than you earn

The most important lesson is probability spending less than you earn — Derek Sivers

It sounds like an old cliché, but it isn't, being able to accumulate is the foundation of wealth, it is not wealth by itself, but the seed of wealth. The ability is derived from being able to offer more value than the amount consumed.

Being able to accumulate demand that you master your basic emotions, people tend to spend more, because they believe that their value in society is determined by the things they own, this couldn't be further than the truth, your cost is determined by your emotional intelligence, knowledge, education, and experience.

Financial freedom is achieved by the simple fact that equity is being accumulated, that equity liberate you, once you have attained the liberty of not caring of what society thinks of you, your financial freedom is bound to become a reality for you.

Equity that isn't serving society will work against you; that is why one must cultivate the knowledge of how to invest; this is a skill that takes time to master.

Money that sits is eaten away by inflation, but when you buy an asset, it tends to be a hedge against inflation.

Investing requires that you offer value to society, that is why the economics system takes care of these elites, people who think only about themselves will get weaker, this isn't a coincidence.

So, because of spending less than you earn, will create a surplus, this surplus will result in acquiring new knowledge, this knowledge will be turned into experience and wisdom.

Chapter 17: The 1% law

Genius is one percent inspiration, ninety-nine percent perspiration

— Thomas A. Edison

I don't remember in which book that I read this, but it has always been beneficial. When I screen the website to find a real estate property, the first thing I look at is how much is this property worth on a gross revenue basis. I take the monthly gross income and multiply it by a hundred, which give me the approximate value that it should be selling. If the seller asking price is close or below the amount that determined, then I start a detailed analysis.

The formula goes like this, take the monthly revenues of the real estate property and divide that number by 1%. It gives you a value of how much should you pay for the property, and it helps to see if the property is worth going further into or passing directly to another deal.

Example, say a property makes 2 000$ / month, well you would divide that 2 000$ by 1% = 200 000$. It is approximate value that it should have, now say the property is selling for 300 000$, well you not even take the time to look further into the property, you move on to the next deal. Now, let's say it is selling for 180 000$, well now you would take the time to analyze even further into the deal.

Now we would take the time to look at the cap rate other fundamentals that would help to understand the real value of the property. I have a great book on Millionaire Real Estate Investing Secrets that go into more details on how to value a property.

Chapter 18: Mind over matter

Rule your mind or it will rule you — Buddha

Once an idea has been formed in mind, actions are the bridge that connects the formless into its shape envision by the mind. Thoughts are energy waiting to be manifested, and one must put the effort for the desired outcome.

Everything originates from the mind, but only persistence and desire to make reality makes it so.

Once you can see how you will achieve success, it is only a matter of time before it becomes a reality. Manifestation will be done in the same fashion as the person truly wishes or wants to experience.

The chair was first manifested in the mind of the creator, and then it became into our existence; the same holds true for every around us. The house you live in is the collection of all thoughts of society and accepted view of society that become so. It is hard to get the concept, but once you do, it will hit you like a ton of bricks.

We create this world experiences by our thinking and imagination. Imagination changes our world, just like the creators of the past, some believed it was possible to harness electricity, and with vision, it become so, power was always there, but in time, it became manifested in our experience as reality.

Knowledge will help you to develop your imagination; therefore, it is essential to become curious about how the world works. I have always been inquisitive to see how everything is connected.

Chapter 19: Productivity

You may never know what results come of your actions, but if you do nothing, there will be no results — Gandhi

Some never do anything, because they believe that what they do, needs to be perfect, putting content is more critical than none.

I love looking at life through this perception, since we usually don't try anything new, because we believe that we are not good enough, but you become good, through experience, so in whatever you do, you must start somewhere.

I genuinely believe that we should seek happiness in our productive day, I do not think that we need vacations to be happy, I am not saying that we should not take vacations, but what I am saying, is that, we should be satisfied in our days of work, it should make satisfied and joyous to see how we are adding value to our society, even if it is for an employer, we should always try to give more value than the amount that we are taking.

When we understand that the life that we are having right now, is the life that we want to experience, then there is no way of feeling that is someone fault except for ours. When we become conscious of the fact that we are precisely creating the life that we want right, we take a hundred percent responsibility for everything that happens in our life,

When we take responsibility and notice how we are creating every aspect of our life through our thinking and feelings, this gives us a sense of joy and increases our power, remember when your power grows, so will your net value. It is not a coincidence.

Chapter 20: Focus

The secret of change is to focus all your energy, not on fighting the old, but on building the new — Socrates

Today, we are no longer able to focus, and we are overstimulated by social media. We have access to so much information that we do not know what information is useful or has value. We are instinctively readier to receive news, but we are not willing to take the time to analyze if this information was accurate or useful.

Even in conversation, people talk about what they heard on the news, and they do not take the time to analyze if maybe, the press is withholding information that could tell another story and that it would make less worse than what is portrayed.

Most of the time, when I speak with a person, the person is unable to stay focus on the subject at hand, he or she may want to talk about so many things that have no importance to the topic.

So, for me, focus on acquiring wealth is very important. Focus is one of the most significant ingredients to making it and keeping it. Focus requires the ability to take your mental energy and focus it on the task at hand.

Focus is really hard in our society, since everything is pulling our attention to it, we must conscious of the dissipation of our mental energies, this will show in all areas of your life, either in your daily goals or in your net worth, when you track your monthly net worth, this will give you the ability to see if you are moving towards your goals or in your life. I measure my life with something that is measurable, and I personally think that we need metrics to track.

It is straightforward to pretend that things are moving in the right direction. The mind will rationalize your decisions and will tell you lies about why you are not achieving your goals or desired outcome; this relates to truth.

Chapter 21: Emotional wounds

Turn your wounds into wisdom — Oprah Winfrey

Understanding and resolving your emotions are a big step in the process of becoming the better person that you deserve to be. Emotional wounds if untreated will put a hold on personal development. Even if you become smarter, you will not be able to become a better or great social person. I am not saying that you shouldn't become more intelligent. What I am saying is that you should identify your wounds, understand them, live them, and then fix them.

A leader needs to understand and empathize with his fellow, or he will be too demanding and will push his colleagues into severe problems.

A person that solves his issues becomes more aware of himself and thus increase awareness, and he can grow faster than another person since he is a stable person that learned to respect himself.

Chapter 22: Steps to acquire wealth

Step one: save

Step two: invest, learning to make returns and making a positive cash flow.

There are many steps to acquire wealth, and you can save your way to wealth or simple create your way to massive wealth.

Saving your way to millions is doable, but at what price? It could take you a lifetime, ok yes, it a sure way, but it cost you your life; it is worth it. Well, I do not think so.

The second pathway is to save and invest, this way is faster than the first, but unless you are using leverage, it will still take a long time for it to work. You can invest in the stock market, which produces excellent returns over the long run. The only problems are the massive swings in the market, and this can have a toll on the body.

In my experience, the best way to create wealth is either through a business that you buy or design, and it can be a product or service that you offer, it must be scalable and independent of your time. It will give you the ability to work on it, find creative ways to grow, and in the process of building it, value will be created in the process.

This value creation will grow so fast, that it will make your head spin, you will get at a point that you will not understand how you got that wealth.

Chapter 23: Become a producer

If you want to test a man's character give him power — Abraham Lincoln

Most of us consume, from material to food and knowledge, yes you can be a consumer of knowledge. I remember watching many hours of YouTube summaries of books. While I was consuming, I wasn't producing. We need to learn and cultivate the habit of creating.

Knowledge converted into memory is folly; one must translate that knowledge into actions, then this applied knowledge becomes wisdom.

The time that I was taking in consuming and pretending that I was working on my goals, well I was not working on my book, there is only way to produce a book, is by taking the time to write. There is only way to start a business, is by starting it.

Chapter 24: Should you follow your passion?

Patience, persistence and perspiration make and unbeatable combination for success. — Napoleon Hill

Never once in my life, did I make money using this approach. The only time I made money was when I was willing to do what others weren't willing to do.

For example:

I made money in real estate, talk to anyone about it, and everyone says, it's not for me.

Made some money on houses that were sold for taxes, believe me, this isn't easy, it is a very negative transaction that can be very uncomfortable.

Living frugal, this wasn't easy, but it worked very well. And even made money in mutual funds, which was to keep making my money work for me and delaying some purchases. Again, wasn't following my passion, but it worked.

I joined the military when I was only 19, and there again, I hated it, but was able to make high income, so, was able to save a lot of money.

I followed my passion a couple of times, like investing in the stocks market, I failed badly, lost like a hundred k, plus the ability to earn during those year.

So, should you follow your passion, in my quest, it was always the hardest things, that paid the most, was I happy through the process, not still. Even some authors talk about, and obstacles are the way.

You should follow your passion in the sense of the goal, but sometimes, you will have to do things that you do not love or are passionate about to attain the desired outcome.

Chapter 25: Low of attraction

"Thoughts become things. If you see it in your mind, you will hold it in your hand." - Bob Proctor

Lost a significant amount of time in this concept, almost the worst advice ever given, the idea makes you feel like you are the center of the universe and that your mind is the creator of every scenario of your day. This couldn't be further from the truth, life in an understandable fashion, is a lot of pain, deception, and suffering, if you do not accept these concepts, every time something happens, you will think, probably there is something wrong in the way I think, you will never really understand, that life is life, not a perception of a reality that you have created, the faster you understand this, the quicker you will find inner peace, suffering seizes for the person that accept life punches and adapt to them.

When faced by obstacles, don't say, life! Why? What did I do wrong? Ask how I can adapt, become better so that the barrier becomes overcome since you will start to build character. Sometimes correlation may point to an idea but remember, causality and correlation aren't the same. At the end of a causality, the results never differ; if they differ, it is probably a correlation.

Chapter 26: Structure

The war is not won with bayonets, but with effective organization –

Unknown

Most business fail, there are many reasons for this reality, but in my opinion and opinions of many, would be that most business lack structure. Many believe that they should do everything, from accounting, filling their tax form, and doing the job.

Trying to sell, being the employee and accounting for everything will reduce the efficiency of your business, the time you allocate to accounting or working in the industry, you aren't doing what you do best, selling your product or service. So, learning to structure your business correctly will increase your odds of success, since you will learn to delegate and organize the shop.

When structuring the business, you should always have in mind that the end goal of the market, is that it should be able to function, even if you are no longer in it. That way, investors will value the business and will pay a hefty price for profits, since it is considered a passive income generating cashflow.

Chapter 27: Thoughts are energy

The secret of change is to focus all your energy, not on fighting the old, but on building the new - Socrates

Thought are intangible, and the invisible creates the tangible, so everything you visualize in mind, will become.

Desire for the intangible to manifest will create an impulse of emotions pushing you to act.

Matter is energy, and thought is energy, and there are of the same thing, which by the way, power does not take any space in this dimension. Like, you can think of the planet in your head, but it was to make the actual space of the thought, your head would explode.

When energy is organized, it becomes something with a higher state of the conscience. The higher the conscience, the more sophisticated the being can become.

Thought are not bounded by time, it can visit the past, or it can visualize the future, the mind seems to have to capabilities of God, omnipresent.

When visualizing the future, we must consider, that time needs to past for the thought to manifest into reality. There must also be nonconflicting thought, since if so, will stop the manifestation of the last dreams and the process start all over.

Chapter 28: The power to become

An oak seed has the power to become an oak tree. - Tomy Shaw

So many powerful words in that
quote, <u>power</u> to <u>become</u>, is so essential, simply
because in life we become what we want to be, we are
what we are today, but to grow, it is a process that takes
time and faith. Through the process of knowing what
we want to be and putting the effort of becoming,

through the process of learning and adapting to the new habits, we become the person that we want to be.

Like the oak tree, it can only become the fully-grown tree, through the process of time, only time can demonstrate the power that the seed had. Remember the power was always in the grain. The seed becomes what it has always been, time revealed it to us, but a spiritual person does not see the seed, it considers the fully-grown tree through the process of vision.

Chapter 29: Natures laws

You are the average of the five people you spend the most time with

— Jim Rohn

Understanding of averages, everything tends to be at the center of the bell curve, gravity, marks, and people. The center of the bell curve composes of 50% of either from the right or the left. The highest point is only 50%, so in other words, there is no 100% in nature, it is always 50%.

The average be power or gravity; everything outside the center is pulled to the center. So for example, if the proportion of a salary of a particular domain is low, the probability of a person achieving high wages in that sector is very low, or in other words, if one chooses to become a doctor, well the chances of having a high paying career is very high, since the average is very high, at first one might only make 100k, well if the standard is 200k, it is only a matter of time before one makes very close to 200k, nature laws are in your favor.

It can be seen in real estate also if one buys below-average price, well his probabilities of selling the property for higher rates are very high, but the contrast is also right.

Understanding nature's laws, become power, because if a person can control output in a specific domain demand, well that identify is able in a sense to control price.

Chapter 30: The 1%

Genius is 1% inspiration, and 99% perspiration. — Thomas Edison

The 1 percent ahead of the bell curve, they are ahead, because they are aware of the coming changes, they read, and they educate themselves about new social trends.

When the iPhone came out, the one percent tried it, and they could foresee that the iPhone was a great device and decided to invest their money in the Apple stock. At the end of the bell curve, these people are the people that are forced to buy the I phone, because they are out of date, and phone companies are giving them their two-year contract. These people decide to get in also in buying some shares of Apple, but who do you think is going to make some money, the one ahead of the curve or the last one? I think the statement is self-evident.

Chapter 31: Love to read

Not all readers are leaders, but all leaders are readers. — Harry S. Truman

Reading is essential for financial success, especially books that explain how wealth is created. New knowledge will challenge your beliefs, which is critical, since if your ideas are of a sick person, well, your results will reflect the opinions of an infected person.

The day I started loving to read, I was able to learn so many subjects, and it contributed to my overall knowledge. I learn how to build my balance sheet on excel by reading books.

I learned how to invest in stocks and real estate by reading, so many people buy real estate, but are forced to sell, since they are negative on their cash flow.

Chapter 32: Life is an experience

Life experience is the best teacher. — David Letterman

You must live life to its fullest. Failure and success are a process of becoming the person that you genuinely want to be.

Chapter 33: Become a creator

Create the life you can't wait to wake up to — Josie Spinardi

Invent, push the world forward, money is one thing, but ideas are another. To remove competition, you must become a creator, since you are unique in your product or service, this makes the possibility for economic profits, by lowering your quantity sold and raising price. It is usually the definition of a monopoly.

Most are people, when considering on building or buying a business, will look at what seems to be working, like I see many pizza restaurant, so I will start a restaurant, that is about the same, so they compete, thus decreases their price, since, quantity is eaten up by the second and pushes prices lower, which removes the economic profit, so now the owner, to make some money, must become an employee, in order to make accounting profits.

Chapter 34: Learning to get financed

Learning is the only thing the mind never exhausts, never fears, and never regrets. — Leonardo da Vinci

Raising capital is an art, so one must learn how to pitch his ideas to the right people, that can make things happen.

Chapter 35: Only takes a hundred sales

Prospecting — find the man with the problem." — Ben Friedman

A hundred sales of a thousand dollars makes you a million dollars, so you are closer than you think.

Chapter 36: Why is real estate a great investment?

Buying real estate is not only the best way, the quickest way, the safest way, but the only way to become wealthy. — Marshall Field

In the long run, real estate is a substantial investment. If it cash flows from the start, well you're in the money.

Real estate is an excellent investment for many reasons; first, it gives you profits; second, its value goes up with inflation; third, you can deduct amortization to reduce your taxes on profits and lastly, it cashflows.

Chapter 37: Percentage of debt

Rather go to bed without dinner than to rise in debt — Benjamin Franklin

I know that Benjamin Franklin was a bit of extremist, but in a sense, don't get into debt that makes you poorer, like, it's better to be careful on expenses that don't make your life better in the future.

On the other hand, when investing in real estate, well your future income will be increased and usually at a higher rate then the interest, so this is wise debt, but if you buy a luxury car, and that you take on a lot of debt, well this has no sense.

Managing risk/reward can be managed by respecting your percentage to debt ratio. I love to be around fifty percent since it is straightforward to achieve, if I have seven hundred thousand in equity, well I know, that I can have up to seven hundred thousand in debt.

Depending on the type of investor you are, you can choose to lower risk, by reducing the ratio, or if you like it riskier, well you can increase the ratio. By lowering or heightening the quotient, comes with its effect on rewards; if one reducing risk, well, there is a price that needs to be paid. If one takes on more debt, well, his reward should theoretically also increase.

Your percentage of debt also represents your leverage, divide one by your percentage ratio. If you divide one by fifty percent, well it gives you a multiplier effect of two, so your asset is worth twice the amount of your capital.

Chapter 38: Beliefs

Your beliefs create your reality

Beliefs create your reality, so many authors talk about this principle.

Beliefs are really imbedded in a person's head, it affects your perception, so whatever you believe, you will force yourself to see what you see, the same for what you hear. If you think something about how life work, anything that contradicts your beliefs, if unaware will make you angry.

To know what one believes in, he or she only needs to look at their results, like your net worth, education, and health, if any one of these domains are poor or struggling, this could indicate the person needs to work on himself. Result are the fruits of beliefs.

Beliefs also affect perception of life, if you believe that they are plenty of opportunities, then you will be able to perceive them as they come, but if for another instance, you do not think that you deserve them, then you will find many reason, for why you didn't take them.

Our belief is primally formed at a young age, growing up, it can be hard to notice that ideas that we are giving, we usually try to protect our beliefs, so if someone contradicts them, your defense mechanism will kick in, by wanting to defend your beliefs by getting angry at the other person.

Only when a person become open to new ideas, that his beliefs are immediately challenged, leading him to the path of enlightenment, that reality is and no longer a perception of reality.

Chapter 39: Feel and look rich

It's not how much money you make, it's how much you keep —
Robert T. Kiyosaki

People rationalize what they bought, by saying that I feel and look prosperous, I will attract more wealth. Wealth is accumulated through asset appreciation and the accumulation of money.

I personally think that feeling and looking rich are different things, wanting to look rich, will not make you feel or be productive.

Looking and being are too different world, and what I notice is that so many concentrate primally on listening and not becoming.

Chapter 40: Study

It is wiser to find out than to suppose — Mark Twain

People rationalize what they bought, by Study and read about the people that you wish to become. The awareness of what you want to become will transform your thinking, which will challenge your habits; thus, will slowly but surely make you into who you wish to become.

To become, one must first be aware of that idealized self, before wanting to work for an investment bank, one must know what it is, what it offers and what you need to have has education, once you know, you can then choose to become.

Awareness increases your ability to make informed decisions, if you think that working at a job that pays for the bills and you do not know, that if you have a great career, that you will not work for many, but you will work to improve yourself, believe me, the outcome is very different.

Chapter 41: Offer more value

Excellence is not being the best: it is doing your best. — Unknown

The more value that you offer, the more you shall receive.

Chapter 42: Growth

Strength and growth come only through continuous effort and struggle — Napoleon Hill

Plants and animals grow effortless, and there is, in my opinion, a lot of wisdom in this last statement.

Since, when we force something to happen, we aren't using natural life laws, like time for money, represents force, especially if one spends all of it. But in contrast, if one works on time per basis, but learn how to control his finances and invest in long term equities, he is now using growth on his side, then it becomes power.

Real estate is an excellent example of a long-term view investment for growth, the asset gains in value, and in some cases, produces profits plus cashflow. These two last points are going to outpace inflation is managed correctly.

Returns on investment and reinvest are effortless, and thus in accord with power, even inflation is accord with power. For energy to become power, it must be organized and controlled. When you look at your equity, it almost looks like a battery, and your asset represents the positive and liabilities represent your negative pole, the difference between the two, represents your power to manifest.

Chapter 43: Life and experience

Maturity comes with experience, not age — Stephanie Chan

What is life trying to teach us?

Chapter 44: An acorn

The creation of a thousand forests is in one acorn — Ralph Waldo Emerson

A seed has the power to become a tree, a seed cannot force itself to grow faster, only through time, can it become what it is meant to be.

Now we need to reflect, that a successful man, while he wasn't successful already had the power of success, and thus only through time that it became apparent.

Can we say, that the interest of wanting to be successful demonstrate that the person has already the power of success in his being? Since the result unfold with time, and no one can really determine their future.

So, to return to the seed, does it need faith to become a fully-grown tree? I think that the answer is obvious; no, it doesn't.

The tree requires no knowledge of faith and even action on its part, and yet it can become, without any effort, grows into what it is supposed to be since we can only see the result through one factor, time.

Time reveals your true nature, so one must let the flow of life flow, and life will explain who you indeed are. You will become, of what you think about, but only time reveals your thinking to yourself, which, can not belied.

Your life reflects your thinking and actions.

Chapter 45: Inflation and capital accumulation

The desire of Gold is not for Gold, it is for the means of freedom and benefits — Ralph Waldo Emerson

Chapter 46: Specialized knowledge

Gaining knowledge is the first step to wisdom, sharing it, is the first step to humanity - Unknown

Specialized knowledge decreases the capital needed to get started, like for example, Facebook, it didn't need buildings and vast amount land to get started, all it needed, was someone with an idea and the skills to create it, I know, that it looks like I simplified it, but it's only to demonstrate, that the person needed more intangible assets than tangible. Today, with give a lot of value, to ideas.

Also, specialized knowledge gives access to high-income careers, since, it only takes a minimum to live, the excess can be saved and put into generating income assets.

Chapter 47: They don't teach this in school

The function of education is to teach one to think intensively and to think critically. Intelligence plus character - that is the goal of true education.

- Martin Luther King, Jr

We hear this statement a lot, and what I noticed, is that they do teach it school, depending on the sector that you study in, if you study in finance, accounting, and economics, you will pretty learn everything that is learned in Robert Kiyosaki book, rich dad poor dad.

Chapter 48: Take back your power

Now is the time to take back your energy, your power, and your peace. — Unknown

Wealth represents the power that you have amassed over the years, by taking the right actions, if you control and properly manage your wealth, it will show in your net worth.

Sometimes, when I hire a person to work for me, some of them, will accept anything that I tell them, but my intention isn't to become a dictator, so it frustrates me, if you don't take your power to choose what you want to believe, someone else, will be happy to control you. If they control you, then they have received your energy and has become more powerful. Become aware of when you give your power away, this will increase your self-esteem and thus will make you confident, and you will not accept to work for less than you genuinely merit.

Learning to take responsibility, increases your power, if you blame, you are diminishing your strength and even self-worth, since you think that something outside of yourself is controlling you, which is, of the simple fact, that you are letting it control you.

Chapter 49: personal growth

Knowing others is intelligence. Knowing yourself is true wisdom.
Mastering others is strength. Mastering yourself is true power. —
Lao Tzu

The learning of delegation is a learned skilled, simply put, you must learn what gives you the most value and what reduces your values.

If you start to look at some of your behavior, you will start to notice, that somethings that you do, give you enormous value, like learning hot to do mechanics of one car, can be valuable, since you are paying the garage approximately 130 per hour. Many people don't make this kind of money, so when you learn how to do it yourself, well every hour leads to the saving of a hundred dollars.

Today, I don't do mechanics anymore, since I found other ways to make a lot more than a 130$ per hour. Sometimes I tell people, that they need to know, what is the things that they do, that gives the most value, and they say I know that in a second, since they answer quickly, I can already see that they don't understand what I am saying, since, there is a lot of reflections that needs to be done, to truly understand.

Every time, you exchange your time, in any domain, you are always creating wealth for your self, remember, that dollars saved after income taxes, is usually worth twice that amount on your gross income.

Chapter 50: We all have the potential

Potential is priceless treasure, like gold. All of us have gold hidden within, but we must dig to get it out. — Joyce Meyer

Fear stops us from becoming the person that we idealized our self to be.

Chapter 51: Linear and parallel thinking

Thinking is the hardest work there is, which is the probable reason why, so few engage in it. — Henry Ford

What I seem to notice, is that when I take a lot of coffee, it seems to help me concentrate, and make a sequence of the thoughts that I am thinking, but when, I don't take it, my ideas get scattered.

Chapter 52: Mind and body

We are what we repeat do. Excellence, then, is not an act, but a habit — Aristotle

The mind and body are simply tools for the soul.

The mind makes a great servant but a bad master.

The body expresses it itself, but the soul has the last word.

Chapter 53: Understanding karma

How people treat you is their karma; how you react is yours —

Wayne Dyer

You reap what you sow, if you mistreat people, well they will in turn mistreat you.

Love and you shall be loved.

Judge and he shall be judge.

Compared and he shall be compared.

Forgive and he shall be forgiven.

I could go on, but I think we get the idea.

We are all responsible for the life that we get, if you have abundance, it is for the simple fact, that you have abundant thought and actions that have value. When you start to realize that you create your life, you start to take actions that contribute to your well being, instead on concentrating of what you do not love. When you get angry, you usually don't find any solutions to your problem, but when you have faith, you try to find solution and even people that can help you, to acquire the things that you seek.

Some people suffer because they concentrate solely on them self, if they started to help other people, they would notice that their problems isn't that bad. They usually suffer, because the ego believes that they should suffer, and you challenge their ego, it will get angry, since it is in an automatic mechanism and they become unaware of this trait that they have, by then rationalizing their actions.

Chapter 54: Probabilities

The first step is to establish that something is possible; then probability will occur — Elon Musk

To try to understand life, we must first learn to think in probabilities. For every outcome, there is a probability of chances that it will occur at every second.

What are the probabilities that you win the lottery, slim to none, now, what are the probabilities that the win the lottery in next second if the drawing is in two days? Well, it is zero, so when, we want something, we must understand the steps that will help us increase our odds of achieving the desired outcome.

Every choice that you take at every instance, either increases or decreases your odds of achieving whatever is that you wish to acquire. Like for example, if you want to find your soul mate, but every weekend, you get shit face, and end up sleeping with random girls, what are the odds that you find your soul mate, well slim to none.

So, if every weekend, you study and save your money to buy a house, and when you meet that perfect person, you take them to a fancy restaurant, and you commit to that person, well there is a high chance, that you will marry that woman, get my point?

A lot of people want success, but in every instance, waste their time and money. Do you think that the odds of success for this person will be possible? But if, you work for a company, and every time they ask you for overtime, and you say yes, every time they ask do you want to take this course to improve yourself and that you say again, what are the chances that you get promoted? Very high.

The same can be said for when a person wins a significant amount of money, if you look at their average net wealth, their newly added equity is way above the average trend, so either they do nothing, for the average direction to catch up with his wealth, or for the wealth needs to come back down and touch the course. I learned this in investing; if you get a significant amount of equity and that your spiritual wealth hasn't caught, you are more than likely to lose it by making wrong decisions.

In the center of the bell curve, is the highest probability of something happening. It almost seems as if, it was gravity, like in space-time continuum, the center mass, is where everything tends to be attracted.

I've learned this in real estate, when you buy something that is undervalued, the center of the belle curve want to bring it to its center, so naturally you will be able to increase it's value very quickly since the laws of the universe are working in your favor, but other instance, when you buy something that is above the average price, your chances of drastically increases its value in the near is almost impossible, could be possible, but of only a little bit.

In odds, the highest odds of something happening, in the long run, is fifty percent, so when you see something that promises a ninety percent chance of happening, well you already know that in the long term, it isn't sustainable.

Say, you multiply, fifty percent times fifty is twenty-five percent but if you multiply, ninety percent times ten percent, then your odds are drastically reduced to nine percent, of it happening two times in row.

Chapter 55: Distractions

By prevailing over all obstacles and distractions, one may unfailingly arrive at his chosen goal or destination. — Christopher Columbus

It almost seems, that there is a power that wants us ignorant (keeping the masses distracted, with television, social media and sometimes even work) Some say, let life tell you what you should do, but I genuinely don't believe that is wise, you should know what you want, since, if you do not see what you want, someone will sell you something that you do not need, since he has a goal, and his goal is to make a lot of money.

There are so many distractions, but if you know what distracts you, you will be able to become aware of when you are not focused on your goals.

Chapter 56: Clients

By looking at the bell curve, one can know how many people are situated in a specific sector, usually what is considered luxury will become a product for the average and then low-end product that anyone can afford.

Wealthy people are willing to pay the price, MacDonald's serve the majority, their cost are meager, so that anyone with a small budget can afford it, but the problem is that, if you get in business wanting to compete with MacDonald, you will not succeed since you are competing on price basis, if you do want to achieve, you will need to focus on making high-end burgers, so that you will not compete on price but quality, this will give you an edge.

The one percent move the world forward with their immense power (wealth), since power or like gravity, everything and everybody is attracted to it.

Chapter 57: Authority

How does one acquire authority? All my life, I've been struggling with this dilemma; even with a considerable amount of money, I couldn't make people work for me.

Chapter 58: Experiences

All experiences are valuable, but unfortunately, some think that bad experiences are what they call a failure. Failure is part of the success process, and one must learn to welcome failure since it shows that your map of reality wasn't accurate.

In 2015, I had invested in the financial system and had lost about a hundred thousand, yeah, I was very disappointed, but fortunately, I learned this experience while I was still young, trying to beat the market is very hard. Easy money makes you weak, while hard cash makes you durable. I was able to make greats amount of money, just like for example, I already made forty-five thousand in a week, at night I would go to the bathroom and vomit, it was just too much money, that I couldn't handle it.

While on a high of making significant amount of money, I would lose all my discipline, and I would start investing in enterprises that didn't have any fundamentals and no technical supporting my trade, even though I knew that my deal made no sense, I would just look at my position, go lower and lower, which I had the choice to sell at any moment.

Chapter 59: Growth mindset

It's not that I'm so smart, it's just that I stay with problems longer. - Albert Einstein

I've noticed, that investors usually have a growth mindset; they seek to make every dollar work and grow. They typically have long term goals. Have they seemed to be able to understand, that the brain can evolve and that they can acquire new knowledge that will give them an advantage to win at the game of life?

Chapter 60: Income growth

Opportunity is missed by most people because it is dressed in overalls and looks like work. --Thomas Edison

Gross income gives you the ability to get a more significant piece of the pie. Being able to get income growth while keeping expenses at check, gives one the ability to explode profits, if you are the only owner of the shares, then you are able to keep it, on the other hand, if you are a shareholder, and the number of shares outstanding's are low, then the company makes profits, then the price of the stock, will drastically increase in value.

Momentum investor are looking for these kind of stocks, since they have very high price to earnings ratio, but in a sense, since the hype about the cost of the capital might increase drastically, investor are willing to pay any price to hold it right now, which pushes the price of the stock even higher.

Peter Lynch is one of this kind of investor.

When we analyze real estate, in order for revenues to grow, one must increase rents or buy more real estate, the first choices doesn't give you a lot of leverage to improve, since, you can only rise by a low percentage per year, while the second avenue, will require an enormous amount of money for the down payment. It's still amazing but, do you think people would be willing to pay a lot more, if you had a company that was growing it's revenues by 20 percent per year, well the company that is growing at twenty percent per year and that the total market of the sector hasn't been reach yet, well people would pay hundred times it net income, this is the reason, why people spend so much for a fast-growing business.

Chapter 61: Courage

Success is not final; failure is not fatal: it is the courage to continue that counts. — Winston S. Churchill

Every step that is taken will require a lot of courage since fear keeps you in your comfort zone; to keep pushing will need a healthy mindset and willingness to achieve the goals desired. It is straightforward to fall in the trap of believing that you deserve easy money, the law of attracting does work, but it work positively when you have become or have acquired the frequency of abundance, but until then, you are vibrating on levels of laziness.

The laziness can be in the form of thinking, physical or even mentally, it is essential, that all types of laziness and weakness to be eliminated from your life.

For them to be eliminated, you must form healthy habits, once these habits are established, then, you will have become a man of value, and since, you vibrate at a level of being able to create value, well then, amount will be attracted to you.

Chapter 62: Creating Value

Try not to become a man of success, but rather try to become a man of value — Albert Einstein

Value is created by increasing the perception of the buyer of the product, or it is created through the ability to make something useful.

In our new economy, it is more important to create value, then to be valuable. The ability to show the utility of a product will give you the ability to create a demand for your services or product.

Chapter 63: Thinking long term

By failing to prepare, you are preparing to fail – Benjamin Franklin

Chapter 64: Work hard

A dream doesn't become reality through magic; it takes sweat, determination and hard work. — Colin Powell

In order to achieve massive success, one will have to work hard.

Chapter 65: Discipline

It takes a lot of discipline to transforms one time into value, and it is so easy to consume; everything in life is made for you to drink, Facebook, YouTube, even other people books, so one must become aware of how they utilize their time.

Chapter 66: Learning for a purpose

Have a purpose and then learn what you need to learn to achieve your goals, don't just learn to learn, there will be no useful purpose and, you won't be able to create any value for your life.

When you want to write a blog and that you have a subject that you want to talk about and you are missing some information, well then you can read on the topic to help you write, this, in turn, will be useful, thus helping you to achieve your goals.

Chapter 67: Types and sources of income

There are many types and kinds of income, they all have their advantages and disadvantages, so depending on your present salary, on type can become more valuable in terms of net income. Understanding how income is taxed, it will help you to understand which is more worth putting your time.

First of all, there is income earned as an employee, if you do not have a big salary, well your income will be taxed at it's minimum, but on the other, if you make a high income, every dollar earned at the end of your salary will be heavily taxed, which this will push you into other avenues of income.

Another income, self-employed, is essentially the same as an employee, with more deduction, but mostly without pension and insurance for disabilities, when you count intensely, you can see that it would be sometimes more worth it, to be an employee.

Third type, business revenues, this is the utilization of many people to offer a service or product, in which the synergies of the group provides more value than if you were to do everything. Businesses can make multiple millions of dollars per year. To give you an idea, a person working at his account can make hundred thousand per year, but in a business, this same person can produce two hundred thousand and even in some cases a million dollars a year. Incredible how a company can show the value that they can give. So, to conclude, if they make millions, they can deduct all expenses associated with the business, so they get taxed on their net income before taxes.

The ultimate source of income is from investments, most of the time, this is a source either taxed at your taxed bracket, or it can be taxed inside of a business. Usually, it is highly taxed, but you must keep in mind, not the same effort has been forth to receive this income.

Then we have another type of income, which is capital gains, capitals gains are taxed the least, but they come with a high price, risk, there is a lot of speculation in order to make capital gains, when you reduce risk, there is high probability that you will receive the money, but in the end, there is less to spend.

The same with the business, when you make a lot of money, you are highly favored, but in the end four out of five business fail in their first five years, so yeah, ok, you made some money when you succeed but on the other hand, when you are an employee, you can choose a highly paid profession, and if you use your head wisely, you can invest the difference and achieve great results also with less risks.

If you choose to create real wealth, you should concentrate on either increase your ability to make personal income, grow the revenue of the business and the same for investing in risk-free cashflow. The ultimate source is tough to control since the value is dependent on the market conditions.

All sources of income can be controlled, but capital gains are based on probabilities, which means, you could lose all of your investment, thus leaving you penniless, but if you have a great ability to make money, well you will be able to remake your money, not leaving you broke.

Unless you are inside of the company, it will be hard to know or control the value of the stock, but if you are a shareholder of your company, then you can influence the value of your shares, either by selling more or by cutting expenses, theses two actions should convert into profits.

General information

When price of crude oil decreased, airlines companies tend to increase, since their expenses decreases rapidly, thus giving the ability to the company to make profits.

ABOUT THE AUTHOR

I am a real estate investor since 2011, my method is to buy and hold, with positive cash flow from the start.

I have been investing in stocks since 2014, technical trading and some fundamental analyses.

I have become a father in 2015

I have also invested in bonds, stocks, mutual funds and tax liens.

I love to read, I have about three hundred books, either on finance, real estate, spiritual books some on the economy.